My Marriage Secret

Samantha Fortner

Whosoever Press

My Marriage Secret

Whosoever
Press

All photographs by Samantha Fortner

The ideas and suggestions in this book are based upon the King James Bible, and the Living Bible paraphrased.

Whosoever Press books may be ordered through booksellers or by contacting:

Whosoever Press
P.O. Box 1513
Boaz, Alabama 35957
www.WhosoeverPress.com
256-706-3315

Printed in the United States of America

ISBN-13: 978-0615787954
ISBN-10: 0615787959

Whosoever Press rev. date: 6-25-2013

My Marriage Secret

By: Samantha Fortner

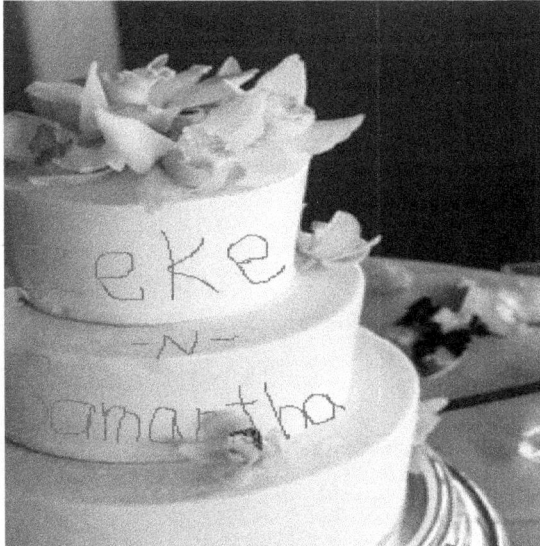

I want to thank my son Nathan Fortner who helped to encourage me to finish this book.

I want to dedicate this book to my husband Zeke and my two children Nathan and Sandra, who were my gifts from God, and you make your mother proud.

Table of Contents

The suggestions in this book are to help you to see the love that God has for us, and the love that we can show to our spouses, family and friends.

Introduction

Happiness is being married to your best friend. Where two hearts become one.

Marriage between a husband and wife the way God said it should be.

I started writing my book after my husband and I were married. I wanted to do something to show that I've done something in my life. I wanted my husband to be proud of me. I wanted my parents and my grandparents to be proud of me.

I was always told by my mother that I had a good head on my shoulders, which made me feel pretty good. So I thought we'll maybe I'm doing something right. My parents had raised us kids up in church from the time we were born, so we knew about God right from the beginning.

They were very strong believers about being at church every time the doors were open. Even if other churches in the area were having special services going on during the week, we were there.

The Early Years

I can remember singing at the front of the congregation after Sunday school classes were over. Songs like Jesus loves me, and this little light of mine, where everyone in the church would watch us singing and clapping our hands.

As I got a little older, I started singing with my stepfather while he played the flat-top guitar. I loved to sing. I can remember my mother saying that at the time I was very small, she would hear me in the back seat of the car or in my room, and I would be just singing away. I can remember always being a happy child. I would sing at home with the cassette player of the gospel groups that would be playing on it. I loved music so much I felt like it was the one thing that kept me going, and made me very happy.

As I entered into high school, I had a dream one night that the church I was attending needed a piano player, and there for a while they were singing without music. So they called on me just at random picking from the congregation to come up and play the piano. I replied with, "I can't play no piano, I don't know how; I don't know anything about it." So they said, just come up anyway, we want you to play, and just do whatever you can do, and make a joyful noise unto the Lord. So I went ahead up to the piano and sat down to play some of the keys, and it just seemed like God's spirit had just filled that place. I could hear everyone singing and I started playing like I knew how to play that piano all along. I can still remember seeing just how my hands were bouncing up and down on that keyboard, it felt so right and it felt so good. It was beautiful, and after all we had a good service.

Then I can remember that it hadn't been too long after that dream when the church down the road from where we lived in Plainfield, Illinois was having an auction and they had this old up-right piano there.

We'll I was so excited to learn that my mother wanted to buy it. So she ended up buying that piano for one-hundred dollars. Boy was I happy. She bought me a book at the music store which told how to make chords and what each key was, and what chords went together. That was a lot of help. And for someone who failed music class in school because I couldn't seem to catch on, I sure did learn this. So I started studying this book and listening to different sounds in songs and how they would change from different chords, and as the months went by I was amazed to know how I had picked it up. I started putting chords together, and started playing some songs. I was so happy. I looked at my mother and said,"Mom I can do this, I can really play this."

I started playing the piano while my stepfather played the flat-top guitar. We would practice on songs right there in the living room of our home. I was playing everything like he was. I thought I was really doing something now. I was so excited, I could play the piano, and that was my dream come true. My mother always said "now you have to learn to play Amazing Grace". That was her favorite song. And so I did.

God had blessed me with playing the piano, and I give God all the Credit and the

Glory, because I know it was him who led me to do this. I love my God, and he has been so good to me, every day of my life.

While I was in high school, we were going to a church in Joliet, Illinois, called the "Highland Freewill Baptist Church." Our Pastor, who was Ken Elkins, would always request for me to sing a song called "almost home."

The day that I was baptized, we had a baptismal service in the creek and it felt like being baptized like Jesus, when he was baptized in the River of Jordan. Pastor Ken Elkins and his father Bro. Frank Elkins, who they referred to as "Tag", who we dearly loved and his mother, they were all just like family. I loved them so much. They baptized me in this creek of water and when I came up out of that water, I came up a shoutin'. I felt so free. I will never forget that time, than they started to sing "almost home." For I know I'm almost home.

I accepted Jesus as my Lord and Savior in September, on the 25th day in 1978. Les Butler's dad, who is Bobby Butler from Indiana, was at the Highland Freewill Baptist Church doing a revival for the week.

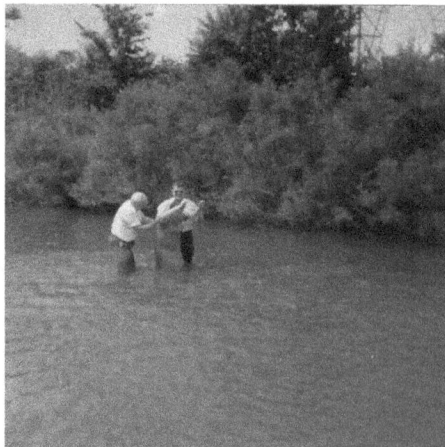

While living in Illinois, Les Butler hosted a radio program on Saturday nights called "crossroads". He played all Southern Gospel Music. I would listen to that program every Saturday night. I wouldn't miss it for anything.

One Saturday night he was giving away tickets to the Inspirations concert who were gonna be in Indiana. We were to answer a question that he was gonna give over the radio. I can remember the question being about the "Hinson's."

So I called in with the correct answer and I won me a ticket to the concert. I was so thrilled; it was the first concert I had ever been to in my life. Once a year everyone would get together at the church when it was time for Homecoming. All the ladies would fix a dish and bring it to the church, and after the morning service we would eat and fellowship with one another in the fellowship hall at the back of the church. While there were those who would still be eating , there would be others to go back out to the sanctuary and pick up a guitar and just play a little, and then soon more would come in and we would all be playing.

We played until it was time to start the afternoon service. I remember for two years that the Spencer Family was there, it was JB, and Barb, and Wade and Kevin. At the time Wade and Kevin weren't even married yet. So you can see it was many years ago.

But we would get out there and start playing music and singing, and I thought this was my opportunity; I want to play the piano with them while they sing, and I did. I had the time of my life.

Almost Home

1. Almost home I can hear the savior calling, Almost home I'll lay these burdens down. I'll hear the trumpet sounding and then I'll be gone, For I know, I'm almost home.

Chorus.

Almost home where the rivers flowing, Almost home where I shall ever be. I'll hear the trumpet sounding and then I'll be gone, for I know, I'm almost home.

2. Children come; I can hear old time singing. Just beyond the Jordan River I'll see home. I'll hear the saints all singing a song of praise and love, For I know, I'm almost home.

"Next to the Word of God,
Music deserves the highest
praise. The gift of language
combined with the gift of
song was given to man that
he should proclaim the
Word of God through
music."

_____ Martin Luther

I am a Christian, and I am going on with my Jesus!

As a child I grew up with some abuse. Then I heard Joyce Meyer speak of the childhood abuse she went thru with. So she was an inspiration to me, she helped me to get through some of my problem areas.

It was helpful to hear that another Christian had the same things going on in their life as I did. I felt I wasn't by myself. It took me years before I could really understand a lot about what had really happened to me. But after going through treatments at the hospital and putting my trust in God I finally made it thru.

When I had first met my husband, all the Freewill Baptist Churches in the area would get together once a month and meet at the roller skating rink to let all the young people have a night out. After going for a few months I started talking to him, and then we were dating, and then you know what happens after that. We became interested in each other and we fell in love and wanted to be with each other.

So we were married on January 31, 1985. I was the happiest girl on this whole big green earth.

Picture was taken October 1984

What the Bible says for the Husband and Wife

For this cause shall a man leave his father and mother, and shall be joined unto his wife, and they two shall be one flesh. Ephesians 5:31

The husband and wife are proved to be one body. Husbands, love your wives, and be not bitter against them. Colossians 3:19

Which say's, you husbands must be loving and kind to your wives, and do not be bitter against them, nor be harsh. They are not a punching bag.

What therefore God hath joined together, let no man put asunder. Matthew 19:6

After creating man, what did God say?

And the Lord God said, it is not good that the man should be alone. Genesis 2:18 I will make him an help meet for him, mans companion.

Then what did God do?

And the Lord God caused a deep sleep to fall upon Adam, and he slept, and he took one of his ribs, and closed up the flesh. And the rib which God had taken from man, made he a woman, and brought her unto the man. Genesis 2:21, 22

How beautiful is this simple but suggestive story...

Now Adam said, this is now bone of my bones, and flesh of my flesh. She shall be called woman, because she was taken out of man. Genesis 2:23 This was the marriage institution ordained of God in Eden before man sinned.

In the Ten Commandments, God has guarded the marriage relation, Thou shalt not commit adultery. Thou shalt not covet thy neighbor's wife. Exodus 20:14, 17

Let marriage be held in honor among all, and let the marriage bed be undefiled, for God will judge the immoral and adulterous. Hebrews 13:4

Be ye not unequally yoked together with unbelievers, for what fellowship hath righteousness with unrighteousness? And what communion hath light with darkness? For ye are the temple of the living God. 2 Corinthians 6:14-16

Ten Commandments for Husbands

1. Thou shalt not take thy wife for granted, but will honour and respect her as thy equal. (1 Peter 3:7)

2. Thy highest allegiance, except God, shall be to thy wife, not thy relatives or friends. (Gen. 2:24)

3. Thou shalt frequently tell thy wife how important and valuable she is to thee. (Phil 2:3) (Proverbs 31:10-11)

4. Thou shalt hold thy wife's love by the same means that you won it. (Song of Sol. 5:10-16)

5. Thou shalt actively establish family discipline with thy wife's help. (Eph. 6:4)

6. Remember to do all the little things for thy wife when you say you will. (Matthew 5:37)

7. Keep thine eyes on thy own wife, not thy neighbors. (Proverbs 5:15-20) (Job 31:1) (Jer. 5:8)

8. Thou shalt make every effort to see things from thy wife's point of view. (Gen. 21:12)

9. Thou shalt not fail to kiss thy wife every morning. (Song of Sol. 8:1)

10. Thou shalt not be stingy with thy wife when it comes to money. (Esther 5:3)

Ten Commandments for Wives

1.Expect not thy husband to give thee as many luxuries as thy father hath given thee after many years of hard labor. (Phil 4:11) (Amos 4:1)

2.Thou shalt work hard to build thy house with the husband that you have, not fantacising about the one that could have been. (Proverbs 14:1)

3.Thou shalt not nag, or hit him with thy frying pan. (Proverbs 27:15) (21:1)

4.Thou shalt cuddle thy husband and be a warm wife. (1 Cor. 7:3-5)

5.Remember that the frank approval of thy husband is more to thee than the side glances of many strangers. (Ezek. 16:32) (2 Peter 2:14)

6. Thou shalt not yell at thy husband but will be a gentle and quiet spirit. (1 Peter 3:1-4)

7. Permit no one to assure thee that thou art having a hard time of it. (1 Peter 5:9)

8. Thou shalt not fail to dress up for thy husband with an eye to please him as thou didst before marriage. (Song of Solomon 4:9-11)

9. Thou shalt submit to thy husband from thy heart and allow him to be head of the household. (Col. 3:18) (1 Peter 3:6) (Eph. 5:33)

10. Thou shalt assure thy husband and others that he is the greatest man alive. (Phil. 2:3)

From the Interactive Bible

www.Bible.ca

What is Love?

There are three stages of Love

1. The Dynamics of Love, it is one of the activities of life, bringing happiness to others, and sharing.
2. The Fundamentals of Love, it is the foundation of love to have faith and trust in each other. To have confidence in myself, before I can place enough confidence in my partner.
3. The Importance of Love, it is that we must open ourselves to receive love and we must be ready to give love.

Learning to Love

"Who are you? What do you want? You may ask, you look awful dirty. I don't even want you by me."

Is that a way to love? NO,

God wants us to help this person, let them have a bath, or give them some of your clothes, show them that you care and you want to help them.

A person who has no love shown to them is as helpless as a little baby. Giving joy to that person may be just what they need to bring them to God.

Little acts of kindness and attention to the people who are sick, or a kind word to someone in need of reassurance, or just finding some time for someone. These may be little things to us, but they are very big things for those who are in need.

So when we love, we need to remember to pray for one another. Prayer has helped many men and women to renew a love that has lost its freshness.

God is the author of love, and comes to the one who prays, and who is showing and acting out love. For a married couple praying for each other is recommended, more especially in the times of a crisis.

Marriage is when we put our love into practice in a whole-hearted manner, so that I can love my partner with my body and my soul. It is often said that love is blind.

But there are four things above all that are necessary for a successful marriage.

1. Passion, which binds a man and a woman together
2. Mental and Spiritual Companionship, as having a common interest, and a

possibility of working together in harmony

3. Personal Love, which includes psychological understanding and respect of personality on both sides
4. As a basis of life, in companionship, there should be a closely related "style of life."

Honor Christ by submitting to each other. For a husband is in charge of his wife in the same way Christ is in charge of his body the church. So you wives must willingly obey your husbands in everything. A man must love his wife as a part of himself, and the wife must see to it that she deeply respects her husband, obeying, praising and honoring him.

Wives fit in with your husband's plans, for then if they refuse to listen when you talk to them about the Lord, they will be won by your respectful, pure behavior.

Your godly lives will speak to them better than any words. Don't be concerned about the outward beauty that depends on jewelry or beautiful clothes, or hair arrangement.

Be beautiful inside, in your hearts, with the lasting charm of a gentle and quiet spirit which is so precious to God. You husbands must be careful of your wives, and being thoughtful of their needs and honoring them as the weaker sex.

Remember that you and your wife are partners. And if you don't treat her as you should your prayers will not get ready answers, and you will have lack in receiving God's blessings.

You should be like one big happy family, full of sympathy toward each other, loving one another with tender hearts and humble minds. Don't repay evil for evil; don't snap back if one of you has an unkind word to say about the other. Instead, pray for God's help for them, and God will bless you for it.

If you want a happy, good life, keep control of your tongue, and guard your lips from telling lies. Try to live in peace. For the Lord's face is hard against those who do evil.

Nevertheless, let each one of you, no matter how good you are, or how bad your spouse is, all husbands are entitled to their wives respect, whether they are wise or foolish, intelligent or slow, skillful or clumsy. All wives are entitled to their husbands love, whether beautiful or ugly, rich or poor, submissive or rebellious.

Nevertheless let each one of you in particular so love his own wife as himself, and let the wife see that she respects her husband. Ephesians 5:33

It is every husband's duty to love his wife, and it's every wife's duty to fear, reverence, or respect her husband, because if she loves him, she will try to please him, and avoid offending him.

A Godly marriage is a bit of heaven on earth.

He must leave his father and mother and be joined to his wife. Genesis 2:24

He must dwell with his wife, and she must not depart from her husband. 1 Peter 3:7

Even if he is an unbeliever 1 Corinthians 7:10

Love is the great reason and comfort of marriage. This love is not romance, but a genuine and constant affection and care for each other, with a pure heart. 1 Peter 1:22

Love Story

Kiss me again and again for your love is
sweeter than wine.

Enchanted by the fragrance of my perfume.
I am as a bouquet of flowers in the garden
of your heart.

For how beautiful we are together. My eyes
are soft as doves, as you look glaringly
through them.

Oh' feed me with your love-for I am utterly
love sick.

With his left hand under my head and with
his right hand he embraces me.

For he is mine, and I am his.

Quotes

A successful marriage requires falling in love many times, always with the same person.   ----Mignon McLaughlin----

When a marriage works nothing on earth can take its place.

You don't marry someone you can live with; you marry the person who you cannot live without.

Marriage, ultimately, is the practice of becoming passionate friends.
                              - Harville Hendrix-

Where there is love there is no darkness.

People who love one another do not dwell on each other's mistakes.

A man without a wife is like a vase without flowers.

My Song That I Wrote

The blood that Jesus shed
For me on Calvary, paid the price
Of my sins for my eternal life,
We'll have a million years to be with him on
That day, I'll be with him on that
Great homecoming day.

For by grace are we saved
Thru the faith of his love
Someday I'll go and be with him in
Heaven above, we'll view that wondrous
place and our friends we all will meet
But best of all, I'll see the one who died for me.

Now everyday gets brighter since I met
him there that night, he's been my friend
when no other one could be,

But I know I'll be in heaven all his glories
we will share; I'll see Jesus, God's only son.

33

Recipe For A Happy Home

4 cups Love   3 spoons Hope

2 cups Loyalty   2 spoons Tenderness

3 cups Forgiveness   4 quarts Faith

1 cup Friendship   1 barrel of laughter

Take love and loyalty, and mix it thoroughly with faith. Blend in with tenderness, kindness and understanding. Add friendship and hope and sprinkle abundantly with laughter. Bake it with sunshine, serve daily with generous helpings.

Note: guaranteed not to fail, if you follow these instructions.

How to Preserve A Husband

First use care and get one, not too young, but tender and a healthy growth. Make your selection carefully and let it be final. Otherwise they will not keep. Like wine they improve with age. Do not pickle or put in hot water, this makes them sour.

Prepare as follows:

Sweeten with smiles according to variety. The sour bitter kind are improved by a pinch of salt of common sense, spice with patience. Wrap well in a mantle of charity. Preserve over a good fire of steady devotion. Serve with peaches and cream. The poorest varieties may be improved by this process and kept for years in any climate.

Rules for A Happy Marriage

1. Never both be angry at the same time

2. Never yell at each other unless the house is on fire

3. If one of you has to win an argument, let it be your mate

4. If you have to criticize, do it lovingly

5. Never bring up mistakes of the past

6. Neglect the whole world rather than each other

7. Never go to sleep with an argument unsettled

8. At least once every day try to say one kind or complimentary thing to your life's partner

9. When you have done something wrong, be ready to admit it and ask for forgiveness

10. It takes two to make a quarrel and the one in the wrong is the one who does the most talking

The Wife

A virtuous woman is a crown to her husband; but she that maketh ashamed is as rottenness in his bones. Proverbs 12:4

A worthy wife is her husband's joy, she is his crown, being discreet, very careful in her speech and actions, having a showing of good judgment, she is wisely cautious.

She is too sensible to do anything foolish, and she carefully does her planning ahead of time. Her husband can trust her, and she will richly satisfy his needs. She will do good to him and not evil, and will not hinder him. But she will help him all the days of her life.

She works late into the night to make sure all is done for her family, works with her hands, and provides the meals for her household. She is like the merchants ships;

she brings her food from afar. She plans the day's work for her servant girls (daughters). She considers a field and buys it, with the fruit of her hands, she planteth a vineyard. She girdeth her loins with strength, and strengthens her arms. Proverbs 31:16, 17 She is energetic and a hard worker. She watches for bargains, she stretches her hand out to the poor.

I can remember when driving to the parks or to the floodwall, you will always most likely find someone who is hungry, or digging in the trash cans hoping they would find something in there to eat or drink. I would keep cookies and crackers in the back seat of my car and when I would see someone like that, I gave them a box and the look on their face when they receive the whole box. They were so happy.

She makes herself her own clothing, and it is beautifully made. And her husband is very well pleased. She is a woman of strength and dignity, having a proud and self-respecting character, being honest, and is not afraid to grow old. She shall rejoice in time to come. When she speaks, her words are wise, and kindness is the rule for everything she says.

Her children arise and call her blessed, and so does her husband and he praises her. A wise woman builds her house, while a foolish woman tears hers down by her own efforts. Proverbs 14:1

Happy is a woman who knows she has a husband who will protect her. Happy is a man who understands this unique creature called a woman. A woman is a very emotional person. She has these needs that need to be met; it leaves her with a feeling of happiness and contentment. And when she is unsatisfied it leaves her with the feeling of unhappiness and frustration.

There are many different kinds of emotional needs. If you feel good doing something good for someone or someone does something good for you, that makes you feel good, and an emotional need has been met.

But when your spouse does something to meet your needs, you are so happy that you fall in love with him all over again. That is the kind of emotional needs a husband and wife expect each other to meet in a marriage.

When we were married, both my husband and I promised to care for each other. We were in love, and were highly motivated to make each other happy.

There are emotional needs of a woman:

1. The protection of her most valuable asset (her reputation).

2. Sometimes she just needs to be reassured, and she needs you to give her a big hug. (She needs your attention)

3. The husband taking the responsibility for leading the relationship.

4. She fears abandonment. She needs to feel secure.

5. Trust, can she trust him to be honest with her.

6. Her physical safety, a man must demonstrate that he is capable of protecting her physically from the threats of the outside world.

7. She needs to explore her sexuality, and be free with you as a natural woman.

A woman needs to feel that she is special in her husband's eyes. A man needs to feel that he is successful in making his wife happy. So what do women want? They want a man's heart!

Let the wife see that she fear her husband. Ephesians 5:33

What then is the Biblical definition of marriage?

In Malachi 2:14 we see that marriage is a holy covenant before God. Therefore, it is meant to be a public demonstration of a couple's commitment. The husband accepts certain marital responsibilities, such as providing the food, shelter and clothing for his wife, and promises to care for her emotional needs. Marriage was designed for companionship and intimacy.

Broken Dreams

I love you more than life itself

But I'm afraid to love,

My heart is like the fragile wings

Of a tiny little dove.

I'm scared to get to close

I feel that I can't win,

You'll love me for a little while

Then you'll set me free again.

I've lived so long on hopes and dreams

I don't know what to do,

I don't think I can trust my heart,

For it belongs to you.

I know you'll only hurt me

Yet I still keep running back,

Between the paths of our hearts,

There's a worn and beaten track.

You've got my heart held on a string

It's breaking right in two,

Enough belongs to me-to-hurt,

The rest belongs to you.

I know that somewhere in your heart

There is a place for me,

I just don't know how to find it

And there's no way to make you see.

I can only hope that someday

You'll wake up and you'll find

That while my heart belongs to yours,

Yours too, belongs to mine.

_____ Tamra L. Noe _____

Likewise, ye husbands dwell with them according to knowledge, giving honor unto the wife, as unto the weaker vessel, and as being heirs together of the grace of life, that your prayers be not hindered. 1 Peter 3:7

So ought men to love their wives as their own bodies, he that loveth his wife, loveth himself. Ephesians 5:28

Nevertheless let everyone of you so love his wife even as himself, and the wife see that she reverence her husband. Ephesians 5:33

A man must love his wife as a part of himself, and the wife must see to it that she deeply respects her husband by obeying, praising, and honoring him. Now concerning the time of being single, it is good for a man not to touch a woman. To avoid fornication, let every man have his own wife, and let every woman have her own husband, because otherwise you might fall into sin.

Now the husband does not have the power of his own body, but the wife has her right to his body, as well as the wife has not the power of her own body, but the husband has his rights to her body.

Now the man when he finds a wife, he finds a good thing, she is a blessing to him from the Lord. Proverbs 18:22

God didn't give you husbands a wife to be your slave, or for you to treat her badly. He gave her to you to love her, for a companion, so that you wouldn't be alone. And the Lord God said, it is not good that the man should be alone; I will make him a help meet for him. Genesis 2:18

If you can find a truly good wife, she is worth more to you than any precious gem.

There are three Greek words translated into the word love.

1. *eros*- a sense of passion and desire.

2. *philio*- a sense of human affection and concern.

3. *agape*- a love measured by sacrifice.

You husbands love your wife with a self-sacrificing love. An ego prone husband too many times we see husbands slip their hands into their pockets and say, I am the Lord of my castle, or I'm the head of my house, or I'm the big banana around here, and you all better do as I say, I'm in charge of my house. It is God's order that a man sacrifice himself for his family.

How does a man sacrifice himself for his family?

He does it through the support of his family. It is the responsibility for a man to go out and support the family. But anyone who won't care for his own relatives when they need help, especially those living in his own family, has no right to say he is a Christian. Such a person is worse than the heathen. 1 Timothy 5:8

Any man who does not provide for his own family is also denying the faith, and has no right to the authority by God to be the head of the home. That authority is responsibility.

It is the responsibility of the man to watch over the economy of his home and the thrift of the family budget.

Some men have a problem just being a man!
But you are not a man until you are:

1. Ready to be responsible for a mate

2. Ready to be responsible for offspring

3. Ready to be responsible to God

When you have achieved these responsibilities, then you are a man!

How can you expect your wife to pray if you don't pray? It is your responsibility to lead your family in the art of praying.

A woman, who is secure in her love, is a woman who will be secure in her marriage. And happy is the man who understands the needs of his wife.

Isn't it amazing how a fellow will court his girl, he'll come home from work, take a bath, shave, put on shaving lotion, make sure he's got a crease in his pants, get all best behavior, he doesn't talk rough in front of her, always talks sweet, you win her heart and she gives you her love, so you get married and walk down the aisle and say "till death do us part". Now after you've married her, somewhere along the line you've quit courting her, and you start taking her for granted.

You don't dress up for her anymore, you don't put on shaving lotion, you come home dirty, smelly, and sweaty from work, and you want to snuggle up and give her a sweet kiss, and you can't understand why she pulls away from you. Do you know what is wrong with you? You stopped courting her. You started becoming obnoshious in your behavior, instead of that sweet, thoughtful, considerate, boy that she married. Be faithful and true to your wife!

Let your manhood be a blessing, rejoice in the wife of your youth. Let her charms and tender embrace satisfy you. Let her love alone fill you with delight. Proverbs 5:18, 19

The man who commits adultery is an utter fool, for he destroys his own soul. Proverbs 6:32

Husbands, these are the commandments of the Lord. He is not asking you to consider doing this, but he is telling you to do this. Husbands you are to love your wife God gave one woman to one man, it's the same either way! One man to one woman. Seek not to be loosed from one another, but to stay together and make it work! To have and to hold till death do you part. For better or for worse, in sickness and in bad times.

Outside of marriage the bed is defiled and you become a whore monger, and God will judge you.

What the Bible says for Children

Children, obey your parents in the Lord, for this is right. Honor thy father and mother, which is the first commandment with promise.

Ephesians 6:1, 2

Children it is your Christian duty to obey your parents, for this is the right thing to do, because God has placed your mother and father in authority over you. Respect and honor your father and mother, so that all may go well with you and you may live a long time.

Now the word "honor" means an act of respect. When you do not respect your parent's authority, you are sinning against God.

Children listen and learn the importance of trusting and fearing the Lord. Do you want to live a long, good life? Then watch your tongue! Keep your lips from lying. Turn from all known sin, and spend your time doing good. Try to live in peace with everyone. The character of a child can be known by the way he acts. Whether what he does is pure and right.

For in today's world there are a lot of rebellious children, they will lie, and not hear what the Lord has to say to them about their behavior and how to act.

A child's relationship to Jesus Christ depends upon their obedience to their parents. You cannot continually say that you love Jesus, and consistently disobey your parents.

In John 14:15 – Christ said, if you love me, keep my commandments. If you love me, you will do what I tell you to do.

Now one of the commandments in the Bible is, Honor thy father and mother. Exodus 20:12

A question that a lot of children come up with is, "where do my parents get all the authority over me anyhow?" This is a good reason to know why you have to obey your parents. The answer is that God has given them the authority over you. To train you up in the way of the Lord. To teach you God's way. God gives his authority to the husband to be the head of his house, and the wife receives her divine authority over her children through her husband.

Train up a child in the way he should go, and when he is old; he will not depart from it. Proverbs 22:6

Parents train up your children in the way they ought to go, in the way of the Lord. It is your responsibility. Pray for God's guidance and wisdom and knowledge, so that you will train them up in the way they ought to go. Parents, you will be judged for how you train up your children, and your children will be judged for how they obey you.

So listen to your father and mother, what you learn from them, will help you to stand. It will gain you many honors.

If you refuse to discipline your child, it proves you don't love him, for if you love him you will be prompt to punish him. Proverbs 13:24

A youngster's heart is filled with rebellion, but punishment will drive it out of him. Proverbs 22:15

By the looks of the world today many children are not being disciplined, they are not being taught what the Bible says and they are growing up to be rebellious adults, having hatred for other people.

Their minds are being taken over by the power of Satan. They are going to school and killing their classmates and teachers. They are even to the point to kill their own father and mother. Such love that is needed to survive in this world today is not being shown to these children today.

Scolding and spanking a child helps him to learn. Left to himself, he brings shame to his mother. Proverbs 29:15

Don't fail to correct your children, discipline won't hurt them! They won't die if you use a stick on them! Punishment will keep them out of hell. Proverbs 23:13, 14

Discipline your son in his early years while there is hope. If you don't you will ruin his life. Proverbs 19:18

Marriage Reconciliation

Be kind to one another, tender-hearted, forgiving one another, as God in Christ forgave you. Ephesians 4:32

And I say to you that everyone who divorces his wife, except on the ground of sexual immorality, makes her commit adultery, and whoever marries a divorced woman commits adultery. Matthew 19:9

Let marriage be held in honor among all, and let the marriage bed be undefiled, for God will judge the sexually immoral and adulterous. Hebrews 13:4

To the married I give this charge (not I, but the Lord); the wife should not separate from her husband. 1 Corinthians 7:10

Everyone who divorces his wife and marries commits adultery, and he who marries a woman divorced from her husband commits adultery. Luke 16:18

You shall not commit adultery. Exodus 20:14

Or do you not know that the unrighteous will not inherit the kingdom of God? Do not be deceived: neither the sexually immoral, nor idolaters, nor adulterers, nor men who practice homosexuality, no thieves, nor the greedy, nor drunkards, nor revilers, nor swindlers will inherit the kingdom of God. 1Corinthians 6:9-10

Accordingly, she will be called an adulteress if she lives with another man while her husband is alive. But if her husband dies, she is free from the law, and if she marries another man she is not an adulteress. Romans 7:3

He who finds a wife finds a good thing and obtains favor from the Lord. Proverbs 18:22

A woman is bound to her husband as long as he lives. But if her husband dies, she is free to be married to whom she wishes, only in the Lord. 1 Corinthians 7:39

My husband is living with another woman. What am I suppose to do? I'm in shock, it hurts, I can't sleep, I can't eat, I am just literally SICK over it. Why? After twenty years of marriage, I had found out that my husband was having an affair. Since I had found out about this, he has not gotten away from this woman. So he left. I packed his clothes and told him to go. He told me that he needed more time to think about everything. We'll there I was just numb, and in a situation that I couldn't believe was happening. I asked him, how could you do this to me?

Do you know what you are doing? Was there something that I done to you? Did I not do enough for you? But all he could say was, it was a mistake, I know I shouldn't have done it. I was so angry with him I didn't know which way to go, or which way was up. I thought O' God what am I gonna do, I'm not gonna make it. I have never been alone, I have always had someone with me, now I have to make sure all these bills get paid, and I can't quit my job. I was so stressed out, I had no idea what I was gonna do.

I was ready to just walk out and let the bank take the house, because the state of mind I was in, I felt I could no longer carry out the responsibilities of paying the bills. I overdrew my checking account for months. It seemed like I just could not get myself with the program anymore. When I went to my job, I was so depressed; all I could do was cry. I thought if only I could get through these eight hours so I can go home. I wanted to give up. I really just wanted to die. I felt that I wasn't gonna make it.

I was never so humiliated in all my life. O' God how could he have done this to me? I was always honest to this man, I always done whatever he asked me to do. I was always there for him. I really couldn't stand the pain that he was putting me through. I knew the only one who could help me was God. I prayed, I pleaded, and I cried for God to give me the strength and the grace to get through this trying time in my .life.

I filed for divorce, and we had the hearing on August 23, 2007. I paid the attorney fifteen hundred dollars to do this divorce. A few days after the divorce hearing there came a knock on the door. It was him.

The first thing he said as he came in the door was, why did you do this? Why did you file for divorce? I love you, and I want to be with you, but I made a mistake. He said I want you to go and put a stop on the divorce, you have thirty days. Please oh' please go and do this, I beg of you. I am coming home but I have to wait a few months, I have to take care of something first.

I had thirty days till my divorce was final, and I said to him, Are you kidding me? I am not going back to the lawyer and make an idiot of myself. So while we were sitting there talking and crying with each other, of course as always he talked me into doing it anyway. So when Monday came I went to talk to my attorney, and explained to him what I wanted to do. His reply was, "now wait a minute, you mean after all that Zeke has put you through you want to stay in this marriage". I answered him and said "yes that's right, I want no divorce".

Feeling as stupid as I did, I really did not want to do this. Then my attorney advised me that if this is what I wanted then I would have to bring him another five hundred dollars. We'll I didn't have that kind of money, what I had I had already paid out. So later when Zeke called me back, I told him what the lawyer said, And he was going on some more . We'll you already paid him fifteen hundred for the divorce, why can't he just do it, why does he need more money?

So it was the next day, I get a phone call from Zeke's mother. And she say's "Samantha I got the money for you. You come and get this money and take it to the lawyer and put a stop on that divorce". I told her no I am not taking your money. I'm not doing it. Yes, she insisted, so I went the next day and got the money from her, and the thought had run through my mind to just keep the money and not worry about it.

But she said, "Samantha I know that it sounds like I am taking up for him, and yes, he is my son, and he has done you wrong. I also was there, I was done wrong by my husband, but I don't want to lose you as a daughter n law either. I have always liked you, and I love you like a daughter. Zeke will never find a person like you again".

We'll I took the money, and felt bad about taking it, that was an awful big amount to get from her. So the next day I took the money to the lawyer, and I guess he was surprised that I did come back with it. He said, are you sure you want to do this? I said yea, but really deep down inside, I was so angry with him and didn't want to do it.

So the marriage was reconciled on the sixth day of September of 2007.

Now months had gone by, and Zeke kept saying to me I've not got it worked out yet. I need a little more time. I said, to him "how much time do you need"? We'll just give me a few months, and then it was, we'll just give me a few more weeks. Till it got to where it was over three years. I was so upset with him, that if looks could kill he would be dead.

At the time I was not going to church, I was out of the will of God. It came to the point where I just gave up. I was hurting so bad inside, my heart was broken, I was trying to keep a job, I would go to work crying, and trying to hold back the tears.

It wasn't very easy. I didn't want to live anymore. My pain was so severe, physically, emotionally, and mentally.

I was so mentally drained, I thought, God, just let me die, I wanted to die. I couldn't keep up with my bills, I would overdraw every month on my checking account, and I wouldn't eat. Or I should say I didn't eat properly. I could not cope with what was going on in my life.

But God was holding on to me. It just wasn't my time to die yet. I went to my job one day, after my husband was at the house; he knew that I had been smoking. Why are you doing that, he would ask. Why are you smoking? You said that you would never do that. So of course I had said back to him, why are you doing what you're doing? Why are you with her? Why aren't you here with me? I was just a crying just as hard as I could cry. He didn't say anything, and just went out the door and left.

Now it was almost time for me to go to my job by three o'clock in the pm. It was already after one. I thought to myself I have to quit crying or everyone is gonna be looking at me, and they are gonna be asking me why am I crying. I just cannot face them like this. So I took two of my prescription tablets of welbruten, and waited a little while, but I was still crying. So later I took two more.

Then it was time for me to leave and go to work. I had three tablets I took with me. So when I got to my job, I went to take two more tablets, and I seen where one of them fell down in the hole that was in the bottom of the cup holder. So now I had no more to take. Then about an hour later I was feeling like I was on a boat rocking on the waves of the water. My head was just a swimming. I thought we'll I'm not crying now.

I felt pretty calm, maybe too calm now. So after I took my lunch break at seven thirty pm, I was really starting to feel sick. My face was flushed and hot, my stomach was hurting, and I felt like I just couldn't hardly go anymore.

I knew what it was from, but I really didn't want anyone to know I took all of that. And I started getting a little scared. But yet I had the feeling too that I didn't care.

So I went and told the supervisor that I was sick and I had to go. I told her that I wasn't going home; I was going straight to the hospital. I felt that bad. I drove myself to the hospital, and checked myself in, and had told them what I done, and why I had done it. So now I had been in the emergency room for a few hours, which seemed like to me longer than a few hours.

A doctor came in and asked me if I was trying to hurt myself. I said, no, which I knew if I said yes, they would send me away to the crazy house. And I sure didn't want to go there. I told him that I was just trying to stop crying because I had got into an argument with my husband. So when he left the room, another person from the hospital staff came into the room and said, that I was gonna have to be admitted cause with the amount of pills that I had taken, I was at risk of having seizers, and I was gonna have to be monitored all night.

So in the meantime while waiting for them to get a room for me, I called a man who my husband worked with, he went to a Pentecostal church. He and his uncle came to the hospital to pray with me, and they talked with me. They knew what was going on between my husband and me because Zeke talked to them about it. So they advised him that he needed to go back home to his wife.

After they were talking with me and praying, I got to thinking. That if I would have died, I would have met Satan face to face, and I began to pray. The fear that came over me as I lay there on that hospital bed. I did not want to go to hell. I began to pray, Father please forgive me for doing something so stupid. I made a promise to God that I would never do anything like this ever again.

It seemed like they were in my room forever, and I was so glad, cause at this moment in my life, I didn't need to be alone. Finally the nurses came back into my room and said that we now have you a room, and we are gonna move you upstairs to the ICU department, where you can be observed overnight. We need to monitor your vital signs where you took all that medicine.

After they got me settled into a room, and got me hooked up to the monitor, I was amazed to see that I was having hardly any respirations. I saw 2,5,1,0. And I thought right there I was gonna die.

I couldn't lay the head of the bed down because I would stop breathing. I felt like it was nothing for me to just hold my breath and not breathe, because my respirations were so low. So I had to keep my head elevated. I laid there and prayed again, God forgive me, I'm sorry, don't let me die; I was just trying to quit crying. I was angry with Zeke.

The first night I didn't sleep, I was awake all night listening to the monitor beeping. It seemed like it would not stop. The second night, I slept some, and the third night I finally got to sleep all night. But I can remember them first two nights when the alarms kept beeping and the difficulty I had trying to breath.

As I laid there in the hospital bed thinking back on all those pills I took, and the one pill that fell in the hole of the cup holder in the car. I said, "God, you made that pill fall in there, I know it was you". You saved me. I can remember before when I prayed to God, and said, "Whatever it takes Lord to keep me from going to a devil's hell, do it. I am your child, and you know what is best for me. I thank God for allowing me to see the good things he has done in my life.

After I was dismissed from the hospital, I went home and I was in the Bible every day, and praying. I said "God I need more of you". I am hungry for your word. I cannot get enough of you.

I said, "God I am tired of fighting this battle on my own. He gets my hopes up and lets me down again".

My body and my mind have gone through so much emotional stress, and it has been so hard on me. So I'm just gonna give this all to you. Now I realized how true that verse was to me in the Bible. To cast all your cares upon me, for I care for you. I said," God, this case is yours, I give it to you, you said you would fight my battles for me". It is yours, In Jesus name.

So after getting back into the will of God, I have learned a lot, and have gotten closer to God.

We have now been separated for eight years; he comes by at times to check on me. Our anniversary has come by again, on January 31, I pray for him all the time, and ask God to bring him home, but most of all that he will call out to God before it is too late. Man cannot live by bread alone, he needs God too!

The Garden of Love

Love is like a garden, the seed is planted, but unless you work the garden, a strong crop will never grow. Love requires long, hard work.

Love suffers long and is kind, love does not envy, love does not parade itself, it is not puffed up, does not behave rudely, does not seek its own, is not provoked, thinks no evil, does not rejoice in iniquity, but rejoices in the truth, bears all things, believes all things, hopes all things, endures all things.

Love never fails.

Love

is patient and kind,
it is not jealous
  or envious,
  never boastful or proud.
  Love is not ill-mannered
  or selfish
or easily angered.
  Love does not keep a record
  of wrongs.
  It does not delight in evil
  but rejoices with the truth.
Love never gives up.
  It always protects.
Always trusts.
Always perseveres.
Love never fails.

from First Corinthians thirteen

A happy marriage is the
union of two good forgivers

___ Ruth Bell Graham ___

Love doesn't make the
world go round,

Love is what makes the ride
worthwhile.

___ Unknown ___

A husband and wife should keep their marriage pure. Rejoice in each other. Don't just say "I Love you" show how much you care. Be true to each other for all things.

Be kind toward each other, kindness builds love. Love your spouse uncond- itionally; live in peace with one another. Seek wisdom as you live together. If you lack wisdom, ask of God, and he will supply your needs.

God is the one who has joined you together. Be patient toward each other. Don't insist on returning a harsh word that has been spoken. Love your spouse even when he is not acting in love. Pray and wait upon the Lord. Be kind, be patient, and be filled with loving mercy. Therefore be merciful, just as your Father is also merciful. Luke 6:36

Take time to pray for the one you love and for guidance to help you to make it down this road, for you have many years ahead of you. For where two or three are gathered in my name, I am there in the midst of them. Matthew 18:20

Draw near to each other. Don't neglect reading God's word with your spouse. Spend time together getting to know God better. His word will delight you and strengthen you.

God made wedding vows. Protect and honor the promises you've made to each other. Don't let anyone come in between you and your spouse. Learn to hold your spouse, and don't take them for granted.

Be supportive and help each other. If you have made a major mistake in your relationship, don't despair. Be thankful that it's always possible to begin anew.

Ask your spouse for forgiveness. With God's help you can enjoy a more satisfying life together. Speak honestly to each other. Honest words spoken in love will make your relationship grow.

Take time to enjoy each other, spend time together in a quiet and special place to refresh your love for each other.

Ask God for his grace and mercy to hold your marriage together. God specializes in healing broken hearts. Learn to love with your actions. True love grows with the years that bind a couple together after a lifetime of love.

Be patient because of conflicts you experience with your spouse. Don't give up hope. 1 Corinthians 13 will help you put your relationship back on course. You never need to fix the pieces of a broken heart alone. Jesus promised to heal the wounds of those who call out to him.

Every marriage has its own special ups and downs. Hold your spouse close when you face grief together, weep together over your losses. The death of a loving parent can shake you. It may be difficult for you to accept this great loss. But however as you and your spouse grieve together, be thankful that God has given you someone to share your deepest pain.

Sometimes the heartaches in your life will seem like they are simply too much for you to bear. But the word of God promises you that your Heavenly Father will comfort us and hide us under his wings. Sometime it may feel like God is very far away. But in reality, God is near at hand no matter where you are. Remember his promise: I will never leave you nor forsake you.

Say "I Love You" often to your spouse.

Forgiveness

Forgive, forgive, forgive

The three most important words for a good marriage.

Why Forgive?

When you forgive, it takes you from the place of the victim to that of a victor

__unknown__

What happens when you forgive?

The forgiving state of mind is a magnetic power for attracting good

__ Catherine Ponder __

I truly believe that love and forgiveness are two of the most powerful things in the world. Love conquers all. Love challenges and encourages. Love changes things, and with love comes forgiveness.

I had a hard time letting this go, to forgive my spouse for the neglect that he had imposed upon me for the past eight years. I took everything to heart. I was an emotional wreck, and cried many tears for about four years.

Then as I was getting into God's word and was really applying it to my life, I had started learning an important lesson; that forgiveness is freedom, and by forgiving someone you not only free them, but you free yourself, from no longer letting negative feelings invade your heart.

Forgiving someone isn't saying that you agree with what they did or even what they did was okay.

Forgiving someone is releasing yourself from the burden that you are carrying around. Forgiveness is not a feeling, but a choice. Grudges hold you back, but forgiveness pushes you forward. I chose forgiveness, I forgave my husband... Today I am free.

As we look at the word together we will see, beyond any doubt, that there is a very close relationship between forgiveness and the love of God. Do you want your relationship to grow stronger over time?

If you care about your relationship, you'll make an effort, and forgive the small things.

Ten things the Bible teaches us on forgiveness:

1. God is a forgiving God

2. God wants to forgive us

3. We are commanded to forgive

4. We should forgive others, because God has forgiven us so much

5. How we forgive others has a direct relationship to how God forgives us

6. God's standard for forgiveness is much higher than ours

7. Most of our attention should be paid to ourselves, not others. We should focus on our sins instead of others

8. We should not take a record of wrongs

9. A loving person will forgive

10. Forgiveness will show itself in action

So what is forgiveness?

To forgive means that we give up all bitterness, resentment, anger, and malice against someone. Not keeping a record of their wrong doings, but instead treat them with kindness and mercy, and do our best to reconcile.

I harbored lots of anger and bitterness. One day, after realizing that the cycle was killing me, I went to the Bible and read about Christ's instruction to forgive those who had wronged you. It said to forgive,

"Seventy times seven"

If I had to forgive him that much, then it must be for my own benefit. There is obviously a lesson that I needed to learn here, and it had taken me eight years to get it. And it hit me, to forgive.

Forgive as Christ forgave you.

Colossians 3:13 says, bear with each other and forgive whatever grievances you may have against one another. Forgive as the Lord forgave you, and just how does the Lord forgive us?

Fully, unconditionally, willingly, time and time again. This kind of forgiveness is supernatural; it is more than we can do on our own!

The Story of Hosea...

Undying Love

Since the Lord viewed Israel as his wife, he viewed her worship of other gods as spiritual adultery. Jehovah had told Israel from the beginning that he would not share her with others. "You shall have no other gods before me ".

So God spoke through the prophet Hosea. The first thing God ever said to Hosea was to "Go, and take yourself a wife of harlotry, and have children of harlotry". God intended to use the prophet's personal relationship with her as a lesson of his own relationship with his unfaithful people Israel.

God directed him to take her as his wife, and so it was Gomer, the daughter of Diblaim. She became the wife of the young preacher. The early days of their marriage were beautiful as their love began to blossom, and God blessed them with a son, and he named him Jezreel.

After the birth of their son, Gomer became restless and unhappy and became less interested in her husband's ministry. She began to find other things of interest to occupy herself, and spent more time away from home. The dangers are great when a husband and wife have few interests in common. Sometimes he goes his way and she goes hers. But in this story Gomer did not share her husband's love for God. Then Gomer became pregnant again. It was a girl this time, and Hosea was convinced that this child was not his. He named her Loruhamah, which means "unloved".

No sooner had little Loruhamah been weaned, then Gomer conceived again. It was another boy. He named him, Lo-ammi, which meant "not my people". It symbolized Israel's alienation from Jehovah.

Everyone knew of Gomer's affairs. But she still ran off with her lovers. He tried to stop her, but she continued to seek her companions in sin.

Hosea would take her back in loving forgiveness. But she would be off again with another new lover. Then it was said that she was leaving for good this time. "I have found my true love, and I'll never come back again". He loved her deeply, as though she had been taken in death. He longed for her to come home.

We cannot escape the message of his undying love. Hosea wanted to see Gomer restored to his side as his faithful wife.

And he believed that God was great enough to do it.

One day Hosea got word that Gomer had been deserted by her lover. She had sold herself into slavery and had hit bottom. Certainly now Hosea would forget her. But his heart said NO! He could not give her up. And God spoke to him, Go and love the woman who is loved by her husband, yet is an adulteress, even as the Lord loves the sons of Israel, though they turn to other gods. Gomer was still loved by Hosea, and God wanted him to prove his love to her. How could anyone love that deeply?

The answer was right there in God's instructions to Hosea. "Even as the Lord Loves".

The only one who knows the love and forgiveness of God can ever love this perfectly. Christian husbands are commanded to love their wives as Christ loved the church, and Hosea is an example of that kind of love.

So he began to search for her, and he found her. Ragged and dirty, and sick and chained to an auction block. Now how could anyone love her now? But Hosea bought her from her slavery for fifteen shekels of silver, and thirteen bushels of barley, and took her home. And he said to her," You shall stay with me for many days, you shall not play the harlot, nor shall you have a man, and he restored her position back as his wife. Now how many times should a husband or wife forgive?

The Lord's answer was, "I do not say to you, up to seven times, but up to seventy times seven". (Matthew 18:21, 22)

There is no end to forgiveness. We need to love like that, and we need to forgive like that.

Conclusion

This is my very first book, and I have really enjoyed doing it. There were pages where I cried and pages where I smiled. I prayed for God to help me and help me to put this book together, and to help me with words to write, that maybe there would be something I would say that could help someone else who would be going through the same thing I was.

God is our strength if we fully put our trust in him. Apart from him, we can do nothing. (John 15:5) Know that you are not alone. The Lord understands what you're going through and he has promised to be with you in every trial of your life.

I thank the Lord for the salvation that he has given to me. He has saved my soul from a life lost and bound for a devils hell. He has blessed me with the joy of being able to play the piano. I don't position myself to be one who plays the best, I still have a lot to learn, but what I do know God had taught me, and what I play is for his Glory.

He has protected me with his mighty hands of mercy. I was in three car accidents, and he was with me in every one of them. I was neglected in my marriage by my husband, but God was with me every day that I had to go on my own, and try to do everything for myself.

He has been my strength, when I was weak, and trying to go day after day. I would always say "God, help me, help me, help me," and "thank you, thank you, thank you". God you are so wonderful, I love you so much. Thank you for putting up with me and the crazy things that I have done. Forgive me God for the stupid things I've done when I should have done it another way.

God gave me two wonderful children, and I thank him. They have been a lot of help for me. They are my joy, and I always enjoy our times together. I love my children very much.

God has blessed me with a job that I was able to do, so I could keep up with my bills while I lived alone without my husband. God gave me strength day after day to go to my job. Some days I went in tears, and some days I hardly knew if I would make it. But I did. I would always pray that my husband would come home soon so he could help me. I was an emotional wreck, it seemed like I could barely do anything anymore. But God has a perfect timing for everything. We have to learn to wait on him. This brings him honor, and it brings us peace.

The good news is that God promises to give you his understanding in all matters. Lean on him for his mercy and guidance.

So now where I'm at today, and wait as he finishes bringing his belongings back home. I will love him, and build my marriage back up. For forgiveness is indeed what will have to be shown in order for this to work.

I feel as if I was living the life of Hosea in the Bible where his wife was out sleeping with different men, but when she finally got home he forgave her and took her in.

After all, your spouse is the most important person in your life. God makes no mistakes. He puts us together as a companion for one another. To work together, play together, and grow together. We need to try to avoid the little quarrels, and always try to get along, and keep peace between each other.

As for housework or even lawn work, give and take a little. Help each other out with all the chores that need to be done. It also helps for you to get them done sooner, and you can have some extra time for each other.

Practice sympathy, and good humor, have fun together, do something enjoying together, and don't grouch. Show some respect to one another, and don't criticize the other for something.

If you have something negative to say about your spouse, keep it to yourself and just say something nice.

Sometimes we all need something nice said to us. Maybe if we were having a bad day, or don't feel well, a nice saying of something may be just all we need to help cheer us up.

Do not fight with each other, but just fight for each other. Your spouse belongs to you. Build your home on a religious faith with love, and forgiveness. Keep Christ in your home.

Author's Note

I wanted to learn more about what the Bible had to say about marriage, and have a better understanding about a relationship with my spouse.

This is a story of things and how they went in my life, and how God has blessed me, and how he has helped hold my marriage together although I wanted to give up many times. But it took the Grace of God to keep me holding on to what I had.

In Memory of Margaret Jean Fortner

December 16, 1935 – December 14, 2012

My dear mother-n-law. She was mine for going on twenty-eight years. And if there were ever anything I needed or needed someone to talk to, she was there, and she would listen to whatever I had to say.

She will always be missed. When she left us, it tore us apart, but I know she is no longer in pain.

We will always hold her in our hearts. Although you were my mother-n-law, you were still like a mom. You will always be in our thoughts, and never forgotten. If there were anything I needed, all I had to do was ask. I miss the talks we would have on the back porch.

Thank you for all you have done for me!

www.ingramcontent.com/pod-product-compliance
Lightning Source LLC
Chambersburg PA
CBHW060118050426
42448CB00010B/1931